5.95

# Success in Volleyball

# Success in
# VOLLEYBALL

## Don Anthony PhD, MEd
President, English Volleyball Association,
Principal Lecturer in Physical Education
Avery Hill College of Education

*With a Foreword by*
**Peter McIntosh MA**

*Photographs by*
John Barlee

**John Murray**

ST. PHILIPS COLLEGE LIBRARY

# foreword

796.32
A628

The success of volleyball as a game is indicated by, among other things, its increasing popularity in schools. From the point of view of physical education it has certain very distinct advantages: it can be played indoors and out; it can be played by boys and girls either in mixed teams or separately; it does not require elaborate apparatus or equipment; and above all it can be enjoyed before a high level of skill has been attained. However, no game is very satisfying unless it can be developed to a level which requires a certain amount of skill. This is certainly true of volleyball. I believe that its increasing popularity in schools will be linked with a growth of clubs desiring to play and expand the game.

The book explains clearly how the game may be taught and played from the early stages to a high level. Furthermore, the photographs will enable those readers who are, as yet, comparatively unfamiliar with the game to see what the individual skills should look like and how these are incorporated in competitive play. I wish the book and the game the success that they deserve.

PETER McINTOSH MA
*Senior Inspector of Physical Education (Men)
for the Inner London Education Authority*

© Don Anthony 1973

All rights reserved. No part of this publication may be reproduced, stored in a retrieval system, or transmitted, in any form or by any means, electronic, mechanical, photocopying, recording or otherwise, without the prior permission of John Murray (Publishers) Ltd, 50 Albemarle Street, London W1X 4BD

Printed in Great Britain by
Butler & Tanner Ltd,
Frome & London
0 7195 2584 5

## preface

Volleyball is an international game which made its Olympic debut at the 1964 Games in Tokyo. The game was invented in America in 1895 but it was not until 1955 that the Amateur Volleyball Association of Great Britain and Northern Ireland began to take shape. The game makes steady progress in the schools and clubs of this country and, as foreign travel increases, many more people will discover volleyball. I am confident that the game will flourish in this country as it has done in so many others.

Volleyball is a game for all ages, both sexes, indoors and out. Socially and physically it has many advantages over some of the more traditional sports. It demands little space and can accommodate many people in that space. The equipment, a ball and a net, is not expensive. It provides excellent training for sportsmen and sportswomen in every game, and is a thrilling sport in its own right.

I am indebted to several generations of students of physical education who have been subjected to my cajoling and bullying in an attempt to achieve high levels of skill in volleyball. Many have gone on to international honours: at least five of the present national squad of twelve players were students at Avery Hill College of Education, and the national coach, David James, is himself another ex-Avery Hill man. The initial enthusiasm of the men has now communicated itself to the girls in the College and the next decade promises great progress in both the men's and women's games.

I am grateful for the advice given by the English national coach, David James, who also features in several of the photographs. I am also indebted to the national coach for Japan, Mr Y. Matsudaira, and to the Japanese Volleyball Federation for advice and several photographs (2, 4, 43, 44). Thanks are also due to: the English Volleyball Association for photograph 110, Miss Linda Brown and Deansfield Primary School for photographs 108 and 109, Kyodo Photo Service for photographs 42, 107, 111 and the *Observer* for photographs 22, 31, 36 and 90.

SUCCESS IN VOLLEYBALL is a new, up-to-date version of the book first published in the 'Do it This Way' series. As in the previous book, I have tried to keep the text basic and simple. It is intended as an introduction to the game, and if it helps you to achieve success in the early stages you will soon arrive at a level of skill and ability that may well take you on to anything up to international standard. The main thing is to enjoy the game at all levels—and help others to do so too.

D. A.

## Contents

| | |
|---|---:|
| *Foreword* | 4 |
| *Preface* | 5 |
| The court, with players' positions | 8 |
| The net | 9 |
| The game of volleyball | 10 |
| The ball | 11 |
| The teams | 13 |
| The officials | 13 |
| The volley | 14 |
| The service | 16 |
| The set-up | 22 |
| The smash | 25 |
| The block | 29 |
| The dig | 33 |
| Skills training | 36 |
| Conditioning | 60 |
| Tactics | 64 |
| Teaching and refereeing | 70 |
| The major rules | 70 |
| Minivolley | 75 |
| Teaching approaches to modern volleyball | 76 |
| Safety in volleyball | 77 |
| Information | 78 |
| A code of honour | 78 |
| Volleyball success | 80 |

## the court

1. The court shall be 18 m long and 9 m wide, free of any obstruction to a height of 7 m above the ground.
2. The court shall be marked by lines 5 cm wide, which form part of the court area. Indoors, the lines shall be marked at least 1 m from any obstacle and 2 m from any obstacle out of doors. A minimum of 3 m is recommended on all courts.
3. A line 5 cm wide, drawn between the side lines under the net, shall divide the court into two equal halves. This is known as the centre line.
4. In each half, a line 9 m long and 5 cm wide shall be drawn 3 m from and parallel to the centre line, the width of the line being included in the 3 m. This is known as the attack line. The attack zone is limited by the centre line and the attack line indefinitely prolonged.
5. The service area is marked in each half by two lines 15 cm long and 5 cm wide, drawn 20 cm from, and perpendicular to, the end line. One line is along the continuation of the right-hand side line and the other is 3 m to the left of the right-hand side line. The service area shall have a minimum depth of 2 m.
6. The minimum temperature of the playing area must not be lower than 10°C.

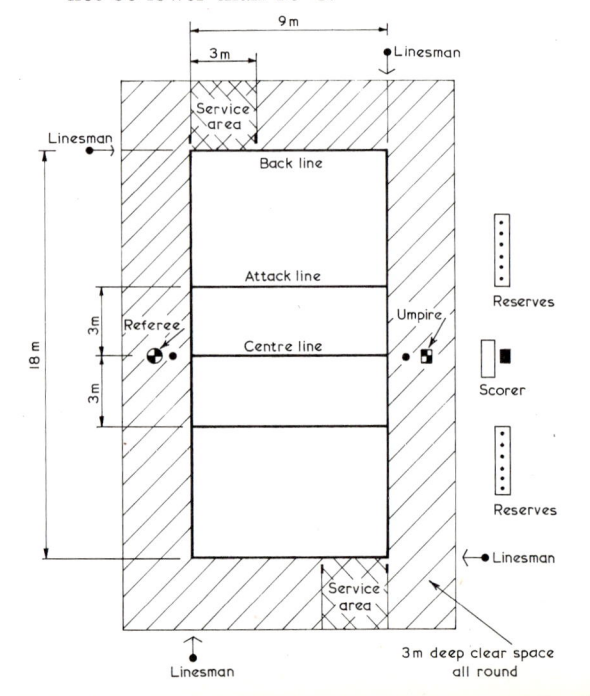

## the net

1. The net shall be 1 m deep and 9.50 m long. The mesh shall be 10 cm and a double thickness of 5 cm wide canvas or linen shall be stitched across the top. A flexible cable stretches the upper edge of the net and passes inside the band of canvas.
2. The height of the net at the centre shall be 2.43 m for men and 2.24 m for women. The height for juniors and children is left to the discretion of national associations. The two ends of the net shall be the same height from the ground and must not be more than 2 cm above regulation height.
3. A removable band of 5 cm wide white material shall be fixed at the sides of the net, above and perpendicular to the side lines.

The net posts must be at least 50 cm from the side lines; they must not interfere with the officials in their duties.

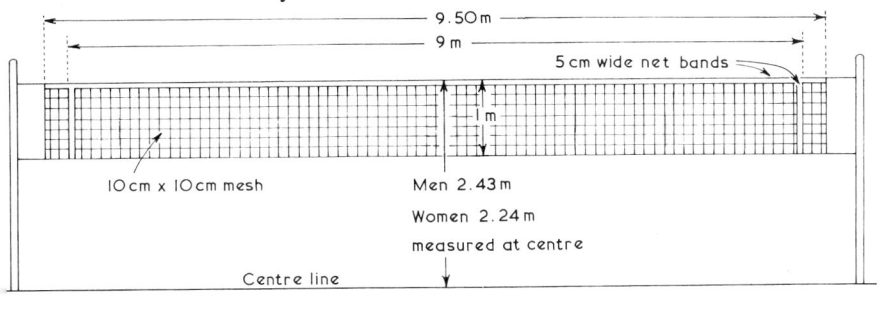

**Note:**
In many of the outdoor photographs used in this book we have not been able to show the ideal tension of a correct volleyball net. You should endeavour to erect a net with strong tension in it so that the ball can rebound in play.

# the game of volleyball

Volleyball is a simple game. It can be played by people of any age and either sex, indoors and outdoors, informally by the family in the garden or on the beach, and formally at all levels up to international and Olympic class. In many countries it is the major recreational game and in some it is a leading competitive sport able to draw crowds of up to 60,000 at international events. It is not a costly game. It is excellent for schools and as a lunch-time activity for factory and office workers. Not only is it a fine game in its own right, it is an excellent training game for athletes, swimmers and players of other games. It requires spring, agility, speed of reaction and timing.

Basically it can be likened to tennis; its main difference is that teams, rather than individuals, play a ball across a net. Each team can play the ball up to three times before it goes over the net provided no player touches the ball twice consecutively (except in the block—see page 29). The game starts when the ball is *served* with one hand by the player in the right-hand sector of the back line. Officially each team has six players, three in the back line and three in the front. Each team tries to ground the ball in its opponents' court and if it does so, or forces its opponents to make other errors (which are explained in this book and in the rules), it wins a point. The team which reaches fifteen points first wins the set. A match is played over the best of three or best of five sets. Only the serving team can score points. If the receiving team wins a rally it gets the service. A player continues to serve until his team loses a rally. When a receiving team wins a rally the whole team *rotates* one place clockwise and the player who finds himself in the back right-hand sector then becomes the server. If the ball touches the net in service that service is lost and the opponents get service.

During play the ball itself, but not the players, may touch the net. As in all ball games there is move and counter-move. The basic move in volleyball is the *set-up* and *smash*. The counter-move is the *block*. An attacking team tries to set-up the ball in a good position for one of the front-line players to leap high and smash the ball down with one hand in the opponents' court. The defending team tries to prevent this move by countering with a block. One or two players in the front line anticipate the smash, jump up and make a 'wall of hands' just above the net—hoping that the smashed ball will rebound off this wall into their opponents' court. The two *attack lines* 3 metres from the centre line in each court are to prevent back-line players from coming up to the net to take part in a block or a smash. They can come inside this line to play the ball however.

Wherever possible in general play the ball is played as in the photographs for the volley (Figs 6–8).

However, it is often not possible to play difficult balls like this, and the *dig*, in which the ball is struck forcibly underneath with one hand or two hands joined together, must be used. *In volleyball the ball may be played with any part of the body above the waist.*

The *dig*, the *volley*, the *serve*, the *rotation*, the *set-up*, the *smash*, and the *block*, are terms used in volleyball. They will be explained carefully in this book and you will be shown how to develop each skill.

Remember this: in volleyball the court movement can become very dynamic but at all times contact with the ball must be *precise*—never rushed and clumsy.

## The ball

The ball must be spherical and made with a leather case, with a bladder of rubber or similar material. The ball

1

2

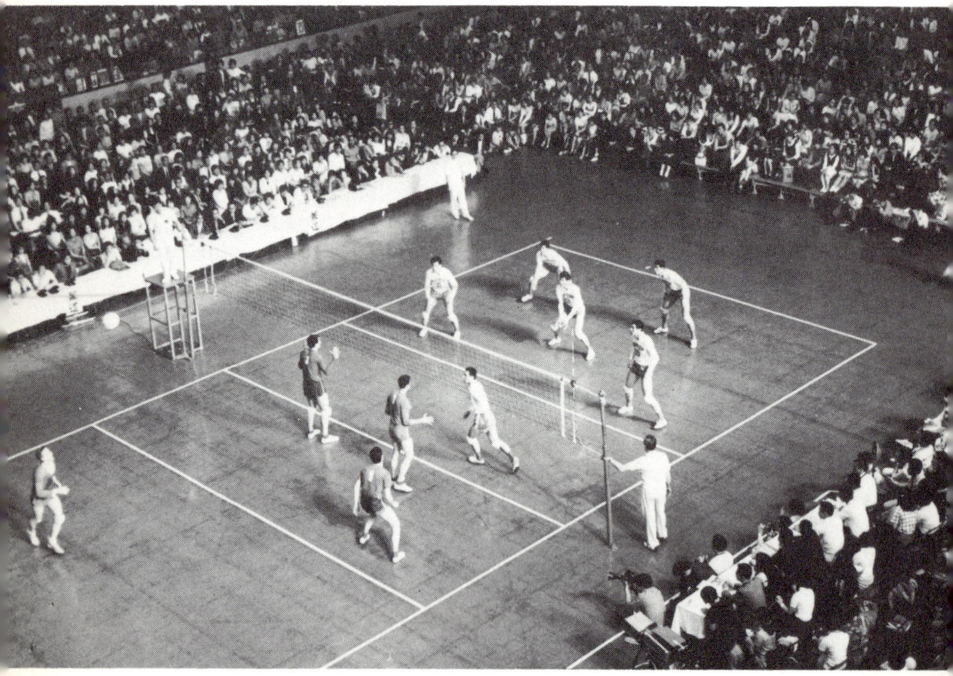

3

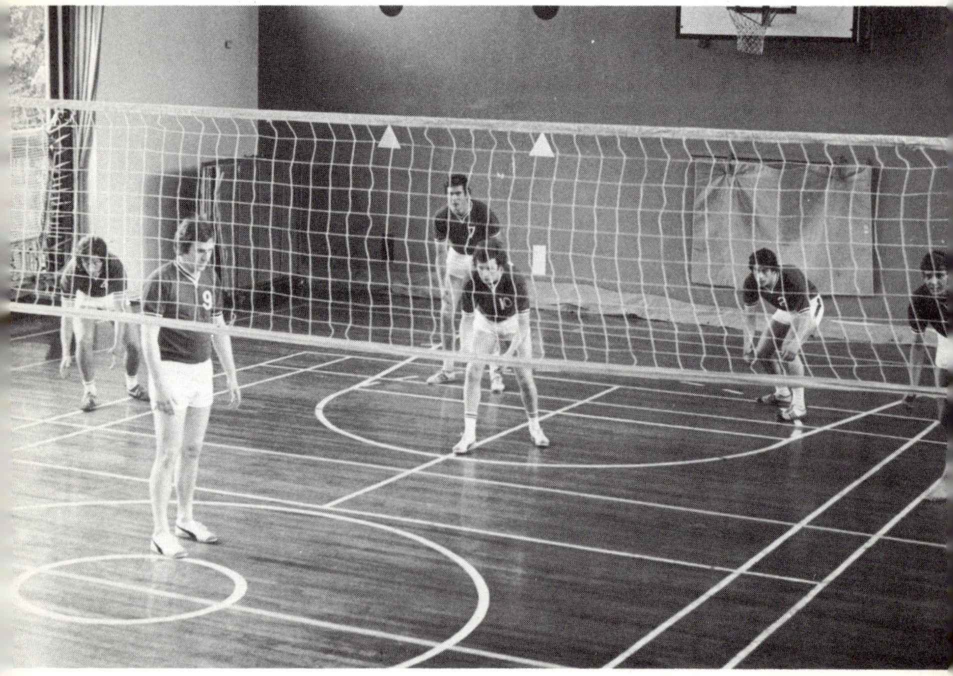

must be of uniform colour; indoors it must be a lighter colour.
Circumference: 65 to 67 cm. Weight: 250 to 280 g.

## The teams

A team is composed of six players.
Three players play in the front line, and three in the back line.
When the ball is served the three front players must be in front of the three back players.
The player in the right-hand sector of the back line serves the ball with one hand, from outside the court.
When the ball is in play the players can move anywhere in court to play the ball, and even outside the court to play a difficult ball.

## The officials

1 Every game must have a *referee* who stands overlooking the net.
2 It is usual to have an *umpire* who sits opposite the referee and helps him.
3 As in lawn tennis two *linesmen* are useful.
4 As in cricket a *scorer* keeps an accurate score.

2 Two teams of six face each other.
Volleyball can be played by men alone, women alone, or by mixed teams.
The referee stands in a position overlooking the net. He is ready with his whistle. The umpire is opposite the referee.

3 Here the team receiving service waits to receive the ball. They are in a 'ready' position. Hands, fingers, arms, legs and feet are all 'alerted'. They must remain in lines of three but they can 'bend' these lines. Notice that they stand in the centre of the court—this is where *most* attacking balls drop. One player is near the net. The others make a 'W' formation.

## the volley

The action you will learn is called the 'overhead pass'. It is one of the most distinctive actions in the game of volleyball, and unless it is learnt correctly the level of skill will remain low. In this book we will refer to it as the *volley*. This will remind you constantly not to 'bat', or 'fist', the ball but to play the *two-handed volley* whenever possible. When you read in this book of 'volleying' the ball back it means using this action. We will talk of 'playing' the ball over the net when we mean the many other ways of returning and playing the ball in a game.

The volley is used in general play, in passing, in setting-up and in playing long high balls to the opponents' back court. It is also used occasionally to drop the ball softly just over the net.

4 5 To learn the correct hand and finger position bend down and place the hands on the ball as in 4, then lift it up as in 5. Now you have the correct position. If the hands were taken away just before the impact with the ball, the ball would hit the middle of the forehead.

6 7 Always look at the ball.
*Move the feet first*—do not *lean* first—to get the body under the ball. One foot should be slightly in front of the other for balance. Bend the knees and then straighten the whole body as you volley. Keep the thumbs pointing backwards to the nose as a general rule.

Relax the arms. Make the movement as graceful and neat as possible.

The thumb and first two fingers give *power*—the other fingers give *direction*.

*Although the ball may be played by any part of the body above the waist*—i.e. it can be punched or headed, etc.—the best and most used action in the game is the *volley*.

It is a good idea to start practising with a balloon and then with a bladder; these are fun to use and slow down the movements. A beach ball makes a colourful second step. Then move on to the proper ball—which is *light* (not a discarded netball or football).

The two hands make a framework and the ball is volleyed from them like a body bouncing from a trampoline. Start by throwing and catching but emphasizing the correct arm and finger positions. As quickly as possible cut down the *catching* action so that there is only fractional contact between ball and fingers. Next receive the ball lightly in the fingers, volley it up a little way and then back to your partner. These little volleys develop accurate control over the ball—practise them constantly.

It is very useful to practise the volley after a ball has bounced. Wait until it reaches the top of the bounce—*then* volley it. It is easier at that stage because it is almost stationary. Also try it lying on your back with a partner 'feeding'.

**8 9 10** The ball is held on the left palm, the right arm is swung back, the feet are parallel to the sideline.

As the right hand swings at the ball the body weight moves from back to front foot and the ball is tossed *upwards in the direction of the serve.*

The ball is struck in flight and the arm follows through.

8  9  10

## the service

1. Service is the action of putting the ball into play.
2. It is done by the right-back who strikes the ball with one hand, open or closed, or any part of the arm, in order to send it over the net into the opposing court.
3. The ball must not rest on the server's other hand when he hits it: it must be in 'flight', i.e. thrown up a little before he strikes it.
4. It must not hit the net: it must pass over the net inside the side-markers (the bands of white material vertically above the sidelines).
5. It must be carried out in the serving area. After he has served the server can enter the field of play.

There are three main ways of serving; they are called:
The underarm serve
The tennis serve
The hook serve

## The underarm serve

This is the most common form of service. It is accurate and easy—an accurate serve is better than a fast one in volleyball.

In **8**, **9** and **10** the server shows the complete action.

If the ball is already moving in the required direction from the tossing action the striking hand has only to give it a little more power to send it on its way. In this method the serve does not hurt the hand. If it is falling back on to the hand as the serve is made it can hurt a little. If you are learning, wear a glove if you like.

In **11**, **12** and **13** you see the different ways of striking the ball in the underarm service. Find which is the most suitable *for you*.

**11** Fist closed and knuckles made as *flat* as possible.

**12** Thumb and first finger pressed close together to make flat surface.

**13** Palm 'cupped' firmly to make slightly curved surface.

**14**

**15**

**the tennis serve**

Here the service is performed as in tennis.

**14** The right-handed player throws the ball up with his left hand. His feet are pointing roughly towards the net and the left foot is nearer the net than the right.

**15** He leads with the right elbow. The body weight moves from back to front foot.

**16** The ball is struck firmly with the closed fist or cupped palm.

**17** The server follows through.

The cupped hand method is more accurate, but beginners may find it easier and more comfortable to keep the fist clenched.

By pointing the fingertips down a little, top spin is given to the ball; by pointing them upwards, back spin is imparted.

The tennis serve needs much practice but when perfected the ball drops at great speed into the opposing court.

When you have found the *technique which works for you*, practise it carefully and repeat each movement of the body exactly, every time you serve in this way.

**18    19    20**

**the hook serve**   This is the most difficult form of service.

**18 19 20 21**   Stand back from the line, feet and shoulders parallel to the sideline.

Throw the ball up from the left hand and, keeping the right arm almost straight (slightly 'hooked' in fact), hit *through* the ball, with a cupped palm.

Follow through in the direction of the opposite court.

Only experienced players can use this serve. This is something at which you can *aim*—in the beginning be satisfied with the simple *underarm serve*. In the overarm forms of serve the *base* of the palm is used to give power —the curved hand to give spin and direction.

Remember—*accuracy* in service is the most important quality—not speed or strength. Try to send the ball into an *open space* in your opponents' court. Always *look hard at the ball* throughout the service.

**rotation of service**

Remember that the same player continues to serve if his team is winning the rallies and scoring points.

When the serving team loses a rally it loses service to the other side.

When a team wins service the whole team rotates one place clockwise so that the player in the right-hand corner by the net drops back to become the server.

**22** No. 1 is leaping high to smash the ball. His team-mate on the extreme left of the picture has *set-up* the ball into such a position that a good smash may be made.

22

### the set-up

This is the action in volleyball whereby the ball is played into a position for one of the attack to jump up and make a smash—i.e. to strike the ball firmly *downwards* into the opponents' court.

The two-handed *volley* is used to make a good set-up.

The ball is played high and about 50 cm from the net. The man in the attacking front line who makes the set-ups is called the setter. Often short people, who cannot leap very high to make good smashes, can become valuable members of a team by perfecting their set-ups.

**23 24 25** In these pictures the player on the right volleys the ball to the centre man who is going to set-up. The setter sets-up the ball into a good position and the first player runs in to smash. This is a common move in volleyball.

Usually the back line play the ball back to the setter who then sets-up for one of his colleagues in the front line.

23

24

25

26

27

28

29

24

## the smash

The smash in volleyball is like that in tennis. Always look at the ball. Try to *copy* the perfect position shown on the next page. It is also like that used in throwing the javelin.

Get high off the ground. Never try to smash unless you have jumped hard off the floor; you must be high enough to smash the ball *downwards*.

After you have smashed concentrate on turning sideways to avoid the net, and to miss the halfway line when you land. Land softly to avoid muscle injuries.

26 27 28 Do not 'peck' at the floor with the toes. Sink down on both feet (which should be flat) and *drive* upwards with the body by driving down into the floor with the feet. Three hoops placed on the ground can help. The approach is then made as follows: first foot in the first hoop, second foot in the second hoop, both feet in the third hoop and drive up and out, landing back in the same hoop. The whole movement is done *rhythmically* to a 'one-two-together and drive' count. Landing *in* the hoop teaches the necessity of not driving *into* the net or over the centre line. As the feet *drive*, the arms are swung vigorously downwards and upwards so that the upswing coincides with the foot drive upwards and greater uplift is given to the body. A right-handed player should ensure that the *left* arm is thrust high in the upward drive.

29 In the beginning have one person *holding* the ball in the correct position while the players jump up correctly to smash the ball off his palm. This is a simple device for getting good form into the jump. Jumping *up*, watching a ball falling *down*, and making a smash action all at once is a complex process for most players at the beginning.

Later, the person smashing *throws* the ball up to the setter and then follows in and jumps while the setter *throws* the ball up for the smash. This, too, is done rhythmically.

30

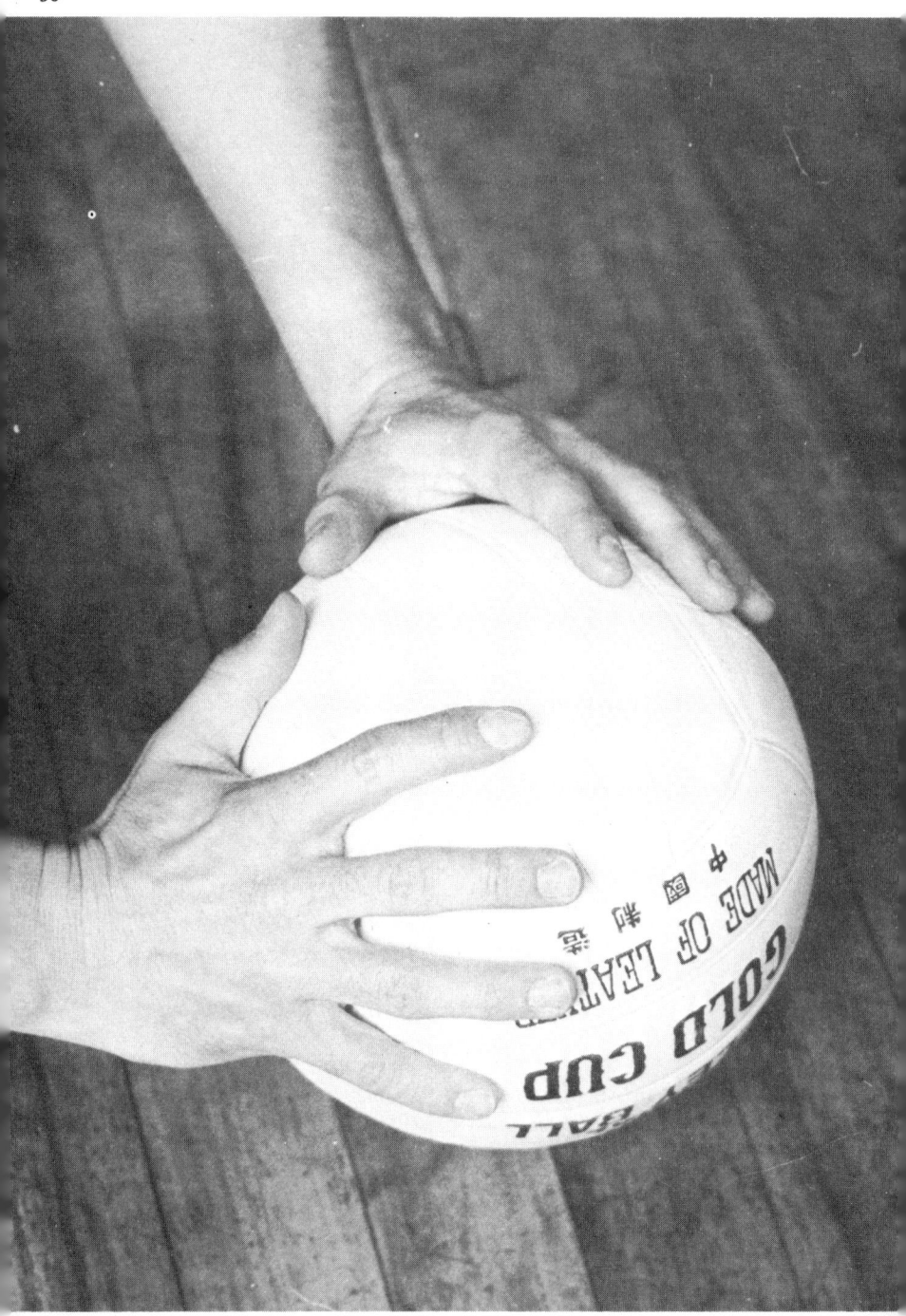

**31**

30 Japanese university champions at the net. No. 8 shows a hard smash.

31 The Japanese girls show that they can also jump high to make a good smash. Notice that their opponents are trying to make a 'wall of hands'—called a *block*. The block is the counter-move to the smash.

All games have moves and counter-moves. In volleyball the standard move is—service receive, set-up, smash. The standard counter-move is the block. This is the subject of the next section.

32

33

28

## the block

The block is an action which attempts to stop an opposing attack. The players may use any part of the body above the waist. It may be executed by the attack players. If the ball touches one or more players who take part in a block it shall count as only one touch. A player who has taken part in a block may *immediately* play the ball again if necessary. This is the only time a second *consecutive* touch is allowed a player in volleyball (see page 10). If a second touch is made after a block it counts as the team's second touch of course. Figs 32 and 33 show how a good block is made.

32 The hands of the blocking players should be 'round' and *above* the ball if possible, *projecting* it downwards into the opposite court. The block in modern volleyball has also become an attacking movement—an attempt to win service. A good block calls for great jumping power. Blocks can be made by one, two or three players. Notice how high the players have jumped.

33 When starting the jump for the block first watch the opponent's feet, then the ball. Do not start the arm swing with a down and up action or you will touch the net. Practise high jumping near the net with the hands *starting* above shoulder height. National coach, David James, shows this position.

30

34 A block is being made by a single player. Note how the players cover the block by being ready to play balls which might get through the blocking hands. In simple volleyball 'covering the block' is done as much as possible by the centre man in the back line. However always be ready to cover a block—and a smash for that matter—wherever you are playing.

35 A block using two players is being made. All spaces on the defending court must be covered and the player directly behind the block must be ready to dive sideways. He must also watch for the masked, short volley over the hands of the blockers.

36 Here the block is being used in an international game. The players are a little too far apart.

**37**

**38**

## The dig

This has become a very important skill in volleyball. For some years it was out of fashion, but is now considered a 'safer' way of receiving service than the volley. Normally two hands are used to 'dig', but on occasions one-handed retrieves must also be made. Normally, again, the skill is utilized while facing the net but might also be needed when the ball is passing the body at the side—and when the ball is overhead and the player finds himself with his back to the net. But do *not* try to move about the court with the hands locked permanently in the dig position! Move naturally—then get the hands and arms into position.

**37 38** Ball hits forearms together—making 'one surface' for contact. Knees are bent and the whole action is 'pliable', not tense. Digging action is controlled: fast balls have the momentum taken out of them. Arms are not used to *strike* the ball like a club. The aim is to take pace out of the ball and project it absolutely accurately—usually upwards—to the player who will 'set-up' the ball for an attack. In early games, however, the ball is 'set-up' by a digging action or returned over the net. Always try to keep the ball between you and its destination. Remember that the position of the arms will determine the height of the ball; the shoulder position determines direction.

**39**

**40**

**41**

42

The one-handed dig

39 If the ball is in front of the body a one-handed diving dig can be played. To avoid injury it is possible to play the ball from the back of the hand, thus leaving the palm downwards ready to start a 'recovery' landing of the flat body on the floor. This movement should be practised without the ball until front dives can be done easily and quietly by taking the first impact on the hands and then letting the body 'bow' so that the impact 'rolls' down the chest, stomach and legs. Remember to try with the 'weak' hand too. There must be a deliberate contact *at* the ball—do not lift and throw.

40 When the ball is more to one side it can be played like this. Recovery is then by a side roll.

41 The one-handed dig often calls for great agility. Here the ball is played from a 'flying' position. Safe landing techniques must be learnt first—good projects for training in volleyball and in gymnastics (see page 63).

42 Excellent technique shown by the famous Olympic Women's Champions from Japan—concentration, fitness, vitality.

## skills training

To enjoy a game like volleyball you must be able to make the ball do what you want it to do. You must therefore practise those skills designed to give you mastery over the ball.

Skills training should also be enjoyable and many skills practices can be made into games of their own in the form of relays and other competitions.

The 'formal skills' must all be done well but there are others and you might work out new skills of your own. Know the traditional moves well but don't be limited by them alone.

In the beginning you might find the official ball too heavy. As we said before, you can start with a plastic ball, a bladder, or a balloon even—and wear gloves if you wish. You will find long sleeves an advantage, and girls may well be advised to tape their finger-tips.

### individual training

Play with the volleyball. Volley it up and down—get it as high as possible—then as low as possible. Volley it—sit down and stand up quickly—then volley it again. See how many volleys you can make in a minute. Volley from one-leg balance position—then from kneeling—from sitting—from back-lying. Volley while running on the spot. Volley it—do a forward roll—and volley it again. Volley—turn quickly on the spot—volley again. There are innumerable variations of this kind. See how many different combinations you can work out.

**43 44** Here you see players in different positions of volleying the ball. The man is getting his body *underneath* the ball and making sure that the ball goes vertically upwards. The girl is trying to volley the ball as high as possible and she stretches to her full extent. You see that people who spend much of their working day in cramped positions can benefit from these movements which stretch their whole body.

43  44  45

**45** A player is trying a skill which has been found extremely useful in teaching the correct volleying action with two hands. The hands are placed in the correct position and the ball is gently caught and thrown with the hands always in this position. Soon the player feels able to make the complete volleying action with the ball rebounding. In this action the ball must hit both hands together (the hands in this action form 'one part' of the body above the waist). If they do not hit together this constitutes 'double touch' and a foul is called.

**46**

**47**

**46** The Avery Hill team is practising diving and falling while making the one-handed dig action. This practice calls for agility and control.

**47** The same team is practising the smash action. The take-off for the smash can be likened to that needed for running springboard diving. To get height and to feel the arched back position in the air the trampoline can be used. In this way you can get abundant height easily and concentrate on the movement in the air.

**48 49** Here another individual practice for the smash is shown. The player throws the ball up with one hand and then leaps high to smash it. This action is useful when you are playing near the net and cannot use a run up for the take-off to smash. It is a movement which calls for good co-ordination.

**50** The same player is working indoors against a wall. He can try to hit a target on the wall to make the practice more difficult.

**51**

**52**

51 The player is practising a difficult retrieving action. In emergencies he might well have to throw himself underneath the ball. This is a good practice which calls for stamina. The player dives under the ball—digs it up—gets up and runs after the ball—then dives under again—and so on, keeping the ball off the ground, until he tires.

52 A good setting practice is demonstrated. The player tries to set into a basketball net. Here competitions can be used—how many out of ten and so on. A second player can then help by passing the ball with the scoring attempt made immediately.

53  54

53 A similar practice is shown for the service. By serving at a wall target or into the basketball net the player develops the accuracy which will enable him to serve into the open spaces of the volleyball court.

54 The player is practising the overarm service and the smashing action. This can be done for length, or for accuracy, using a wall target. It can also be practised vertically, i.e. by smashing the ball downwards on the ground to bounce it as high as possible. Notice how the player keeps his eyes on the ball and follows through in the direction in which he wants it to travel.

*Remember to practise the smash action with both left and right hands.*
Ultimately this practice must be made using the net and full court.

55

56

42

**Pair & small-group skills**

Many combinations and single skills may be practised in pairs and small groups. Again they can be made competitive by setting one pair against the others—for example, by keeping the ball going as many times as possible.

57

55 Shows a combined 'set-smash-dig' practice. This is a very common combination practice.
56 Shows the basic two-hand volley. No. 7 demonstrates how to get the body *underneath* the ball; kneeling is often not enough—you might have to *dive* quickly.
57 Shows pairs practising the catch and throw using the correct volleying finger position. When this is right and both hands hit the ball together try to catch lightly with the fingertips, toss the ball upwards a little, catch with the tips again, and then pass back to your partner. As soon as possible move on to complete and accurate volleying or you might find it difficult to *stop* catching the ball.

**58** Players, in pairs, practising the tennis serve.
**59** A pair practise the two-handed dig—ball being played by forearms contacting *together* on the ball, thus constituting a 'legal' play. If this contact is not precise a 'double touch' will be called by the referee.

**60** One player—the receiver—plays the ball from a crouch position. This is excellent exercise for the leg muscles which will project him up for the smash and about the court at great speed.

**61** The receiving player is kneeling. His partner *throws* the ball to make it difficult for him to retrieve—the retrieving player must get under the ball any way he can and send the ball *upwards*.

Using pairs, all the combinations used in individual skills training can again be used. Players can sit and stand alternately while volleying to each other. They can do press-ups, rolls, jumps and other movements—and all this is very hard physical exercise.

**62**

**62** The players are practising the basic movement in overarm service and smash. They are striving for accuracy and power. The receiving player can either catch and throw or volley the ball back to his partner. Another variation is for each player to try to drive his partner backwards by sheer power of action. This will help to build the strength needed to execute a first-class smash or overarm service.

The skills training for the block shows only the single block action, but three and four players can practise the same movement.

**63** The two players face each other and try to jump as high as possible. They keep the hands about 15 centimetres apart. They see who can jump highest. Then one makes his run, take-off and jump—the other tries to follow all the movements and block his hands. As a variation they can lightly touch fingertips.

**64** The same practice is made using a ball. One person stands or jumps holding the ball. The other pats both hands on the ball. Then they make it competitive, with the player holding the ball trying to avoid the person making the block.

**65** The players then join forces to make a pair—blocking the attack of a third person. A fourth person can also be involved to 'set-up' for the 'smash'.

63 64

65

47

**66** The players show a very good set-up practice. Since set-ups are often made from positions very near the net, practices must also take place from this position. The pair volley the ball to and fro, trying to control the exact position of the high point.

**67** This shows the progression to the set-up and smash. The player on the right of the picture has passed to the centre man; he sets up and the first player runs in to smash. This favourite practice can employ the whole team who form a line facing the net. Each man in turn passes to the centre man who sets up for each man in turn.

**68** The players volley to each other from the sitting position. This action might be useful in play when the player has to fall backwards under the ball to volley it upwards accurately. In this practice he learns to roll back safely. Later they might practise this from the crouching, and then from the standing, positions.

**69**

**skills training in circle formations**

There are many practices from the standing, sitting, jumping and lying positions using the circle formation.

69 Three players show a simple volleying practice. They could do this while running on the spot, and only play the ball after jumping, i.e. playing the ball while the body is in the air. They could also turn about and play the ball to each other by passing backwards over the head. The backwards pass is useful in set-up movements and sometimes as a defensive measure when a player finds himself with his back to the net; he must decide quickly whether to volley backwards over his head, or dig. In these practices it is fun sometimes to have two balls in use. In the beginning it is advisable to let the ball bounce once before getting beneath it to volley.

**70** A very difficult practice is shown. Here the team make a running circle. They play the ball upwards and each man in turn runs underneath and keeps the ball going. The secret of this game is to set the ball *high and vertically upwards*—not backwards. In fact the ball should merely go up and down with the team running underneath one after the other.

A similar game can be played by each player volleying the ball up and down for a few steps on the run, before setting it high for the following player to run underneath and take over.

71

72

73

**74**

**'spry' work**

Most of the volleyball skills can be practised easily in the 'spry' formation, i.e. when one player faces a line of the others and the ball is played back to him by each player in turn.

71 A spry activity with players sitting.
72 Mixed group work outdoors. These games can be made competitive with one group matched against the others.
73 The two-handed dig being practised in spry formation.
74 The one-handed dig.

Similarly all the skills of the game can find their place in this practice formation.

**relay work**

It is easy and enjoyable to work out simple relay games using volleyball skills.

75 Two teams face each other and players work across from team to team passing the ball. Two groups like this can work against each other for fun and competition.

There are many relays using the team and counter-running principle. Teams can run up to a wall and volley or smash against a target, catch the ball, and run back. Just think of a relay you use, and try to fit a volleyball skill into it.

There are also several interesting games using the 'follow on' principle against a wall.

76 Members of the Avery Hill team show how they use a wall in skills training. Here the players are volleying high against a wall running away to the back of the team while the next man follows on to volley—and so on—keeping the 'pot boiling'.

The one- and two-handed digs can also be developed usefully with this practice.

76

**77**

**line of three skills practices**

Many skills practices can be worked out using a line of three players.

77 The players show the basic line-up.
The left-hand man can volley to the middle man.
The middle man volleys back to the left-hand man.
The left-hand man then volleys right over to the right-hand man.
The right-hand man then volleys to the middle man who has turned about.
The pattern is repeated several times.
The players change places.

Another variation you might try is:

The left-hand man volleys to the middle man.
He volleys back.
The left-hand man volleys over to the right-hand man and quickly moves forward to change places with the middle man—he now becomes the middle man.
The right-hand man volleys to the new middle man.
The new middle man volleys back.
The right-hand man volleys over to the new left-hand man, and changes places with the middle man.
And the pattern is repeated constantly in this way.

These are complicated patterns of movement and you will find it best to start by *throwing* the ball to each other.

Using the same formation as in 77 we can try another game.

The left-hand man volleys to the middle man who volleys over his head to the right-hand man, and quickly changes places with the left-hand man.

The right-hand man now volleys to the new middle man who volleys over his head to the left-hand man, and quickly changes places with the right-hand man.

This pattern is repeated time and time again.

Finally here is another line-of-three skill invented by the Avery Hill players.

The ball is volleyed from player to player down the line and back again but the right-hand player in the photograph must run from end to end as *he* has to make *both* ends of the line. The player running must work very hard as the other two do all they can to wear him out.

78 Here No. 1 (right) volleys to No. 2 (centre) and sets off immediately for the other end of the line. No. 2 volleys over his head to 3, and 3 volleys overhead to 1—who has reached the far end. Nos. 2 and 3 turn about and the ball is now played in the reverse direction. This continues until the running player is exhausted. The players take turns to be runner and the winner is the one who can keep going longest.

**pressure training**  All games players now use the system of training called 'pressure training'.

In this system games skills are practised under conditions far more arduous than the game itself. If the skill deteriorates, stop.

78

**79** One player is throwing the balls as quickly as possible to the next player—who tries to make a good high set-up. The fielders roll the balls back quickly to the thrower. The thrower must make the setter move about and play the ball from difficult positions.

**80** Here is a similar pressure training activity. Here each player has a ball and throws in turn to the centre man who tries to play the ball back accurately; the team keeps up a strong and speedy pressure by throwing the balls in quick succession.

To make this more arduous the centre man must play the ball only when his feet are off the ground, hence he must keep jumping up and down while continuing to play the ball. This is a physically exhausting activity.

**conditioning**

**81**

It is quite clear that the good volleyball player needs to be in excellent physical condition.

He or she must run, and walk daily, and do gymnastics for agility and suppleness.

In addition there are several exercises that help volleyball directly.

81 The Avery Hill team are doing press-ups on the ball to develop finger strength mainly; stronger fingers will make the volley action better.

82 The team is playing volleyball from the crouch position on a hard tennis court. This is a lighthearted variation but strong exercise for the thighs.

83 Here a player is building the leg power needed for good jumps as in the smash action. He is jumping with a weight on the shoulder. If he cannot jump he merely squats up and down. *In all movements like this he uses his legs and keeps his back straight.*

82

83

A great problem in volleyball is court movement. Players tend to be rooted to their spot. Good volleyball rests on fluent court movement. This can be 'felt' by letting teams play soccer-tennis and, if there is adequate ability, head-tennis. Both games call for whole body movement. This tends to transfer itself to volleyball if the teacher tries hard.

**84**

**85**

**84 85** The players show the use of a high bar to develop spring they jump up and try to look over the bar. This helps them in the jump *vertically upwards* which is essential in volleyball. Jumps upwards and *forwards* near the net mean that the chances of touching the net—and thus fouling—are high.

**86** Training for the front dive-retrieve dig. Take the weight, after digging, first on the hands then on the chest, followed gently by stomach, thighs and feet. This can be done absolutely quietly and safely after much practice. Use mats in the beginning.

**86**

**88**

**87**

**89**

**87 88 89** A player shows how to recover after a dive or a fall to retrieve the ball. In advanced play much diving about, often on hard floors, is called for, and this method of safe recovery must be practised. Remember to *roll* on the back and shoulders. Do not put out a hand and arm to stop the movement—this leads to arm fractures and dislocations.

Training for this should mean that the player returns always to his starting position. After starts from a static position, go on to rolls from walking and then running starts. Go both ways. This is excellent conditioning.

## tactics

In volleyball, as in all games, there are tactical moves to practise. In the beginning these moves can be better worked out by throwing and catching the ball.

When you move on to actual volleying it is useful to play on a tennis court; you can also allow one bounce between volleys if necessary.

90 Here we are reminded again of the speed and power of the international game. All players are concentrating and are in postures of readiness, both teams trying hard to work out successful moves and counter-moves. Tactical play means being a move ahead of your opponents. The question we ask ourselves is: how can we outwit our opponents? The attacking player is attempting to beat the block by cleverly 'flicking' the ball with one hand. This is a very difficult skill and unless performed superbly it will be called a foul for 'carrying'. This skill is sometimes called the 'tactical ball'. The block can also be beaten by a player feigning a smash but changing to a volley at the last minute—so projecting the ball *slowly* over or round the block.

**91**

**92**

91 In the team with service the front three stand *near* the net ready to make a good block after opponents have returned the ball. The centre man in the back line is the player best able to shout directions. Sharp, clear directions of this kind are essential in volleyball. 'Mine', 'Yours', 'Out' cries will avoid the fatal *hesitation* which spoils the early stages of the game.

92 The receiving team waits for the ball. It is often useful in early volleyball for the centre man in the front line to stand *near* the net. The others try to dig or volley the ball back to him so that, on the second play, he can set-up for an attack.

93

94

95

66

**96**

**93** The ball has arrived.
One man is forward to be setter.
The team play the ball to him and he can then set up to other attack players.

**94** Here you see the middle man volleying the ball to a setter who is on one side of the court; he can set to players on the other side of the court, or in the middle.

**95** No. 8 has passed to 4 who has set up for 5 to smash—this is the common orthodox tactic in volleyball. Note that all players try to *cover* each other, i.e. they try to anticipate anything that can go wrong with a move and prepare to help out. *Three-touch volleyball* is vitally important. Dissuade teams from lazily volleying back on the first or second play.

**96** Two of the opposing team have managed to get up to block. A third player is *covering* the block. No. 7 is *covering* the smash. Keep alert and mobile. Never rest your hands on hips or knees.

97

98

99

68

97 All eyes are on the ball—the ball is falling vertically and a player is preparing to leap high to smash.

98 The dark-vested player gets up to smash—the white players prepare to block. Note the player on the left of the picture with his hands on his knees—there should never be time for a position of rest like this in volleyball!

99 The player setting is passing the ball overhead in an attempt to deceive the opponents—who expect set-ups to be in the direction he is facing.

100 No. 4, the left attack player on the far side of the net, has made a 'feint smash' to disturb the opponents, as his colleague on the right makes a good smash. See what faults you can spot regarding the 'cover' of the defending team (answers below).

100

With tactics as with skills, this book introduces you to only a few of the many involved in volleyball. But this is the joy of the game: once you have mastered the basic skills and can control the ball, volleyball can be enjoyed with a very limited knowledge of tactics. Tactics, however, pave the path to progress.

Player on extreme left should be further right
Player next left should be further back
Player extreme right should be further back.
All three should be in 'ready' position

## teaching & refereeing

Always keep the game as *simple* as possible.

Don't be too strict in the early stages; get an enjoyable game going and introduce the rules slowly as the players get better. The art of enjoyable volleyball-teaching is to keep the game going—in the beginning, *keeping the ball off the floor* is the main object of volleyball. Allow any number of touches to start, then five, four and lastly three.

Don't be afraid to lower the net. Letting the ball *bounce* once in the early stages might help good teaching.

Allow the server to throw the ball at first, and then to serve from halfway.

In serving teach the method which pays off best for the individual; go for accuracy rather than power.

Introduce the skills systematically and associate them with a 'games situation' as soon as possible.

Many of the skills practices and conditioning exercises will fit into the 'group activities' section of the physical education lesson. They can also be organized in the form of a circuit; circuit training based on volleyball movements can be very hard work.

## the major rules

The next three pages deal with some common points about volleyball rules.

**101**

**102**

101 The dark ball is the only ball 'out'. As in many other games the ball that is 'out' must be *completely* out. A ball *on* the line is *in*.

102 A player shows how it is possible to run *outside* the court to play the ball. However, the ball must always pass back over the net between the white side-markers on the net.

**103** A player demonstrates a foul; he touches the net. To foul the centre-line he must step *completely* over the line (New Rule, 1972).

**104** The player clearly touches the net in trying to block the smash—this is also a common foul.

**105** A player reaches *over the net* to play a ball—if the net is not touched this can be allowed, especially in blocking (New Rule, 1972).

**106** A double-foul is shown; when this happens the point is played again. A player on each side has touched the net.

**107** An exciting moment in a Japan *v* USSR game. Volleyball can be full of dynamic movement like this.

**switching**  This is a term to explain a tactic whereby, *after service*, for example, the players in the front line can 'switch' positions so that a good 'setter' might move to the middle, changing places with a good 'smasher' who will get into a better attacking position. A player from the back line could move forwards to 'set', thus allowing three potential 'smashers' in the front line.

**substitution**  As in basketball, every volleyball player is allowed a substitute. Every one of the six players has a substitute. A substitute can come on *once* in each set.
Substitution is used in top class volleyball. The keen players should read all the rules about this and about many other technical aspects of the game.

## minivolley

In some countries—following the developments of 'five-a-side soccer' and 'minibasket'—the game of minivolley has been instituted. It is a game particularly suited to younger children or beginners.

Recently the International Volleyball Federation has asked for the standardization of minivolley rules, especially as they apply to the 9 to 12 age group. The principal object is to 'adapt the game to the needs and capabilities of young beginners'. Here is a summary of the main points:

1. A team consists of three players and two substitutes. They position themselves so that there are two front-line players and one back-line player. The back-line player serves the ball.
2. The playing area shall be 4.5 m wide and 12 m long. The height of the net shall be 2.10 m for both male and female teams. The ball shall be the official volleyball or a plastic ball having the same dimensions and weighing 220 grams. There shall be a serving area of 1.5 m in length.
3. The refereeing policy should be roughly to 'adapt the rules to the level of skill rather than vice versa'. The rules are, in general, as for the normal game, but a full set of them is available from the English Volleyball Association.

**108 109** Children from Deansfield Primary School in South London try minivolley.

## teaching approaches to modern volleyball

Good teachers can make *all* the skills and skill practices involved in the game of volleyball challenging, progressive and enjoyable. The exercises and drills suggested in this book can be fitted into most lesson patterns. The search for both improvement and excellence can be satisfied. In common with other games, volleyball can be easily introduced by following the general principles employed in modern games teaching. In brief these are:

1. Use imagination in utilising spaces and equipment:
   The gym can be divided longways by using a long rope on wall hooks; this provides for several small games crossways.
   
   Beams lowered to a suitable height, a folded trampoline, and any other available 'crossbar' can be used to provide a 'net'. Practise setting at wall marks or into basketball rings.
   
   A lighter ball should be used for beginners; a bladder or beach ball in the first stages; then a light plastic ball before graduating to the volleyball proper.
   
   The height of the net should be flexible—a height at which most of the class can just 'smash'.

2. Use common sense in enforcing the rules. Let players reach fair levels of skill and enjoyment before insisting on exact techniques and rules. In particular allow a 'thrown' service in the early stages—otherwise games never get going. Also allow more than three touches at the start— 'keeping it up' and 'getting it back' are the two most important principles for beginners.

3. Many teachers today prefer a 'game centred' approach. The six *v* six game is approached gradually through one *v* one, two *v* two, three *v* three and so on; these smaller games are played on proportionally smaller courts. Techniques can also be 'limited', e.g. games with volleying or digging only, or 'dig-set-smash'.

## Safety in volleyball

Volleyball can be played indoors, or outdoors on grass, playground or all-weather surface areas. Wherever it is played the surface should be smooth and clear of stones and other debris. In frosty or wet weather grass areas may be unsuitable. The area of play should be properly marked and indoor courts should be positioned so that adequate space to the sides and to the rear is allowed. Side and back lines should never be close to walls or other obstructions.

Under certain circumstances, such as when introducing practices to beginners, a rope may be substituted for a net, but for later stages an appropriate volleyball net should be used. Supports for the net or the substitute rope must be secure. Free standing posts, such as netball posts, or unstable wall fittings must not be used.

A lightweight plastic ball is most suitable for practices. A heavy leather ball with prominent lacing or welted seams can cause unpleasant injuries to the skin. A proper volleyball is best.

Players should be lightly clad and plimsolls should be worn. Heavy shoes are not suitable and could be a hazard to other players.

The game should be supervised properly. Players must not attempt to pull or swing on the net.

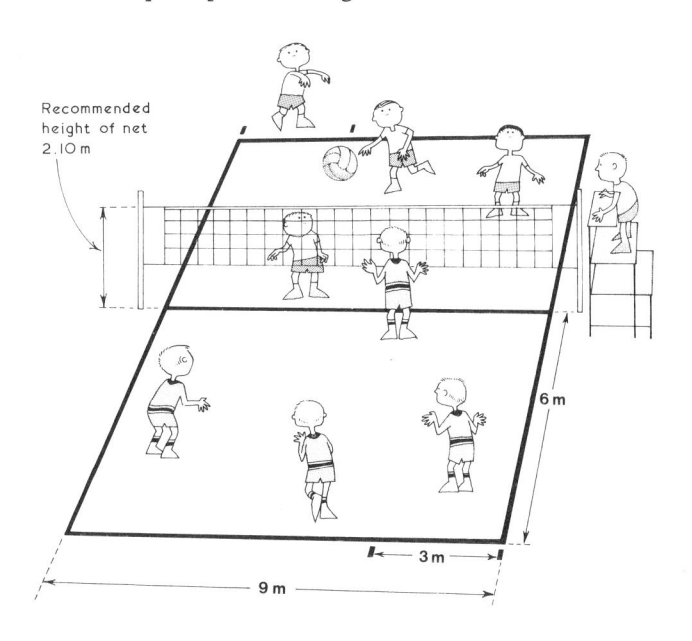

Recommended height of net 2.10 m

6 m

3 m

9 m

## information

The governing body for the game in England, Wales and Northern Ireland is the English Volleyball Association (EVA). Scotland was originally part of a joint Association but has now established the Scottish Volleyball Association (SVA) separately. For Olympic affairs the British Volleyball Federation (a small committee) has been constituted. Both the EVA and the SVA are affiliated to the International Volleyball Federation (FIVB) with headquarters in Paris. In all areas of Britain there are regional volleyball associations, leagues and championships. There is also a National Schools Volleyball Association for boys and for girls. England, Scotland and Britain enter teams of men and women for international competitions and there are national leagues for the best clubs. More than 100 countries play international volleyball. The results of the 1972 Olympic Games were: Men—Japan, German Democratic Republic, USSR. Women—USSR, Japan, Korean Peoples Republic.
The EVA publishes a Journal and administers courses and qualifications for referees and coaches. There are coaching awards at elementary and advanced levels. Information on rules, available films and film-strips is also provided by the EVA; scoresheets and copies of the rules are also obtainable.

For full information on membership and services write to
Mr T. Jones General Secretary
English Volleyball Association
Dartford College of Education
Oakfield Lane Dartford
Kent

Mr J. Close Secretary
English Schools Volleyball Association
22 Baret Road
Walkesgate
Newcastle-upon-Tyne NE6 4HY

Scottish Volleyball Association 4 Queensferry Street Edinburgh EH2 4PB

A full copy of the International Rules of Volleyball can be obtained from the General Secretary of the English Volleyball Association, or from the Scottish Volleyball Association.

## a code of honour

Fair play and sportsmanship are fundamental to this game—as in all others. Always be *first* to admit a foul at the net or in play.

110 England *v* 'All Stars', Wembley 1971.

111 Japan *v* USSR, 1970.

**volleyball success**

This photograph shows the speed, agility and concentration needed to play international class volleyball

GV
1017
.V6
A53